# Freedom, an Explanation

by Faizan Mufti

I0447441

"It is the power to think, speak and act without externally imposed restraints and in its p ristine form is the immunity from all duties and obligations"

All this which I am writing is because of the fact that everyone wants ind ependence in every aspect of life but none so far has defined what truly i s unrestraint, that attaining it will give complete liberty forever and will s et a standard of liberty of which nothing less will be accepted of,

An Idea that no one is bound by any laws, code, moral or ethical obligati ons to do anything that he does not want to do and can in no ways be co mpelled to do as is otherwise considered an obligation binding upon him according to the belief of others,

 and to be made to follow a code of limitations that to which the individua l doesn't submit to is nothing less than coercion and the in violation of th e person's personal identity even though the identity itself is the result o f multiple persuasive forces which came in contact with the individual an d he found some more alluring than others,

although the idea of limiting liberty so that liberty is also insured for oth ers has its strong valid justifications but it only comes in effect when oth er's liberty has been taken and it suggests no ways in which every indivi dual is guaranteed complete independence and in between ensuring that other's independence is not limited as it goes far as to curb independenc e more and more so that the possibility of another's independence being taken away might arise so it is crucial to limit everyone else's independe nce from letting anyone have chance to limit anyone else's independence  and then that limited independence is considered the ultimate independe nce and this process keeps repeating and repeating and everyone's perc eption of the bar of liberty get lower and lower

and will lead to liberty being so constricted that the society will rise up a ll together and with its non-defined term of liberty will make barbarianis m the norm because as there was nothing which clearly defined liberty d uring the time when it was not as curbed as it would be in the later time without the clear cut view of complete independence without risking any one else's is by ensuring just one word LIBERTY

<u>The Three Syllables</u>

The 1st Syllable: Liable Idea

- An ideal is not responsible for its followers but the followers are responsible for their ideals

The 2nd Syllable: Be Expecting Return

- No one is to be compelled into submitting to another's ideals by the direct use of force and if anyone does that then everyone else has the right to use force against him

The 3rd Syllable: To Yourself

- Everyone has the right to do anything with that which he owns or those who agree themselves to do as he says and it should not affect others that which they own or else the matter would be decided according to the affected one's judgment

<u>Accept</u>

Consider these principles are considered as the new three syllables of Li
berty,

And are fought for whenever seeking justice and nothing less than this b
e accepted at any cost will usher in a new era of enlightenment where all
 other orders will run side by side and being run on only those who are
willing to let themselves be run by it, giving each individual such an enor
mous list of choices to choose from even though this change will give ris
e to a new form of ideological market in which the ideals of an individual
will be precious as gold but this market will be very volatile and will pre
vent any group from getting a complete monopoly over it as its said in th
e 1st Syllable even a single stain in the characteristics of those who uph
old the idea will cause the ideals own collapse, this system will ensure th
at even if the a person outnumbered by a million or more in a region wou
ld not be directly forced into the ideal of the remaining population, As, "
An idea which cannot solely defend itself on the basis of  peace is not w
orthy to be even be considered"

"This Idea is not in itself an ideology but the idea which will make all oth
ers ideologies possible"

These little struggles that will come into effect after the Great Realizatio
n, Will turn grow powerful and powerful and will bring about a ripple effe
ct which will eventually gather such force that it will remove the titles of
 ultimate supremacy, suitability and acceptability in all times at all places
 from all those claiming such,

 all those resisting to the suppressing orders will encounter all those opp
osed to their struggles as nothing less than their arch enemies they on th
e other hand being backed by all those that possess foresight and see th
eir repressive ideals being crushed and will brand the liberators as traito
rs to their homeland or simply put a bird trying to free itself from its cag
e which the hunter has designated as its own and deluded everyone else
in there into not escaping this menacing system of political entities whic
h everyone must owe allegiance to and love the one where he was born

and filling everyone's mind with such absurdities as telling them the othe rs are not like You and You are by the grace of whatever You believe in are lucky enough to be born in a perfect society that by the miracle of Y our presence seems way better and has the best ideals then everyone el se as they are different from You think differently than You and look not hing like You while in reality in  every society even though they express their views and actions in a different way the driving force their emotion s are all same all feel the same cold are burned by the same fire and hur t by the same stone and with only the removal such artificial bounds as b orders ideologically distinct nations and people, will everyone see that Y ou and them are all alike.

Only the influencing ideals that are dominant in the presiding region hav e made You believe differently and there is something unique about ever yone not even two grains of sand are alike You are special in Your own way a jewel in the world without which the world would not be like the w ay it would be and that would be nothing without You as every drop of w ater made ocean so You Yourself are a part and a completely unique, and  without You this idea will be nothing You are a community in Yourself an d the idea dies within the community as it stops believing in it,

 once You realize what liberty is, no force in the entire existence will be powerful enough to change the main its fundamental concept it will allow  You complete independence to do as You wish with all that You wish to do it with provided You own it,

 for complete liberty it is essential that all power hungry system relinqui sh control to all that they without any right claim to be owners of meanin g all public property must be abolished no institution or individual be allo wed control of that which it cannot manage

 as in the old orders all unoccupied lands are claimed by the so called ma sters who have deluded entire masses into accepting them as governmen t with or without their consent leading to unrest and eventually rebellion s no other person be allowed to act for all without all of them explicitly a greeing to complete subservience with their own free will,

As for making the corrupt old orders give right to free choice the move ment for personal independence will not remain peaceful as they will not bear that which their minds cannot comprehend and they ensure will all t heir might that this demand for the basic right be crushed at the very be ginning

both mentally and physically and only Your steadfastness can save it and their level of getting things done by direct force must not be adopted at all even until the very end and even if You become strong enough and re alize the power rests not with them it's not them holding the balance its You holding it and them too altogether

it's Your own conscience that have kept things from falling apart where as they think not with their heads until their fists become weak and then they change barbaric repressions to a little less barbaric and even after so much time they have not done anything to allow personal independenc e as it goes against their own personal gain as once any individual realiz es that only their limitless desire for repression of everyone who is not t hem is at stake their entire might combined will not be able to break that persons will even if he couldn't be independent physically he'll forever b ecome independent mentally and the world that the way it looks will feel completely new,

Extraordinarily progressive ideals will turn up and all the scientific advan cements that have been halted as they might risk their profits will come t o light and the individual will no longer debate on how he should be ruled but will become his own master breaking away all the chains of confine ment, making each and every one forging their own path instead going in one that one has been forced to walk, this idea is nothing like anything e lse it gives unrestraint to the absolute limit while completely maintaining order, it not only gives complete physical and mental liberty but also allo ws everyone a fair share of wealth giving even the most poorest in term s of wealth a chance to start a new life without the obligatory sum being extracted from them unless they themselves give allegiance to an order requiring such or make up their own, with such flexibility being given to each and every one of You and will give You the power to the create the world as You see fit and inviting everyone else to Your way of life makin g their life as better as You've imagined to make it,

## You

This idea of liberty is the summation of complete perfection and there is no other idea comparable unto it, and it's Your job that this realization be explained to everyone else making You a courier of liberty, You must go and tell everyone of this. making them be their own masters like what You have just now become, and You'll Yourself be the founder of the new era of liberty making everyone independent as the birds that fly up high they being so magnificent in their journey, You can Yourself shatter all these imposed bounds on Yourself if not for other as every action is as great as the existence as it echoes forever and ever through every particle there is just like the beating of Your heart don't ever underestimate Your own potential. You are just as good and potentially even better than the best men that ever lived as Yourself is the complete embodiment of all that which You have ever came in contact with,

Ponder over all Your short comings and find out for Yourself whatever is better for You, for the life of land is not fit for the creature of the sea, the ideals that are better for You, may not be better for someone else and vice versa, realize Your uniqueness and others as well as You are as unique for them as they are unique for You,

No one can really see one's uniqueness if they themselves do not want to see it improve Yourself and once that improvement is complete in You encourage others to do the same,

Once You the torch bearer of this idea have perfected Yourself then all others will look to You for exceptional way of life, the way of life an independent mind that is not compelled into submission by force no matter how much force is applied against it

As You Yourself are responsible for Your ideals and You should make sure that Your ideals must be so exemplary that there must not be any problem if those are accepted as way if life by all others,

You Yourself must make Yourself able to see past that which is not true but is appeared to be so as even the darkness itself is nothing more than the absence of light and evil itself is nothing more than the absence of g ood and all these depend upon the perception of an individual as events a re as good or as bad as perceived by emotions

Even those emotions are the result of the long term indoctrination upon an individual and when once that individual starts to look beyond what ot hers have told him to be the ultimate truth many aspect of an event begi ns to unfold in front of his very eyes and he becomes astonished at all of this that how he could have missed I, how did he not see it when it was right in front of him,

and that truth he so dearly cherished to be infallible and without any err or when it turns out not to be so all his expectations are shattered befor e his very eyes and then and only then he realizes that nothing is true an d everything is permitted and all those that made him believe otherwise are in their own graves without owing even a cent debt to him as he him self allowed to be deluded this can only be prevented when You Yourself look at the multiple aspects of the matter at hand and question why that which is, the way it is, how did it come to be so and what will happen ne xt and considering all possible outcomes its consequences and rewards a nd what must be done,

## Follow Yourself

Forge your own path and follow not blindly those who did the same, become Your own personality the way You seem it will work best for You but force it not on others as You'd not like them forcing the same on You work towards Your own well-being and before You know You'd have perfected Yourself so much that You'd not even believe that You were once not so perfect as You'll be latter.

Don't take things for that which they are but for that which they can become as even the most precious pearl can be made in the most invaluable oyster, as You only by a little effort can make Yourself perfect so by a little bit more You can make the entire world that way You must not stop at any cost be the best at whatever You do continue doing that which You started and don't be lazy, as even a parrot who has learnt to talk is way more valuable than the one which hasn't

Follow the example of time which itself doesn't stop and continues the way it does without the care of anybody else's opinion as the world will only try to say no to You, will tell You, that You cannot might not and will not do anything extraordinary becoming more and more aggressive with every success You gain, don't try to interpret their response as they themselves don't mean what they say as they themselves are making their opinion clear to You make them Your opinions clear and continue on continuing that that which should continue and don't be too busy thinking that You forget to act and don't be too busy acting that You forget to think realize the real lies with Your real eyes. look at what You should do depending on what's going to happen and not based upon what had happened as the past itself was made only by looking to the future by doing that which was not done before.

## Free Yourself

All the old orders have been made on the assumptions of formulating a u topian society by mixing their new interpretations with the old and gettin g only their inspirations by what had happened and forcing their ideals o n others as they themselves think it'll make their life much better where as force always lead to destruction, orders that need force to support th eir way of thinking only created unrest among the populace and led to ev en more chaos and trying to restrain people from doing what they want o nly because of the fear of them dooming themselves have led to much de struction and their mistake of control which they use to curb possibility o f chaos makes chaos reality as only one spark is required to burn the ent ire hay stack,

To do that which needs not be done is as not doing that which needs be done, and the main reason for work is its reward and there always exists a risk in everything even trying to be completely sane carries the risk o f being completely insane, even in the most perfect of state their exists c haos and the similitude of the all the old orders is nothing more than one who is preventing a baby from learning to walk as he might fall during t he process, messing things up is not bad at all but not knowing what to d o afterwards,

All the old orders try to force a utopian society not knowing how to achi eve it and not even knowing what to do if achieved they have no complet e understanding of what they preach or follow, as a beggar would not kn ow the pain of losing a car where as a rich .man would not know the joy of being content, everyone strives for diverse ends and forcing everyone to work for the same thing eliminates the very basic nature of humans t heir emotions which determine what should be done and gradual influenc ing is way more effective than swift force.

## Know Yourself

The most important thing to understand is that happiness is different for everyone some people's vision of utopia is having a loving family and watching their children grow up, While for others it might be to live a life of wealth and fame forcing eithers vision of utopia upon an another will create only sorrow,

And inability of achieving that which one wants will make one detest the order that which is preventing him from it and true utopian society can only be made when each and every individual is completely allowed to live the way it wants a perfect example can be found in the inert gases of chemistry as they don't react with other elements and are a perfect utopian society among themselves as they let not others force them into anything nor do they force the others into their way if this example is adapted by You, You simply become happier and happier as the key to happiness is caring less and less the less You indulge Yourself in other people's businesses the more content You'll be, as You won't care to force Your ideals on another so will the others might do the same and this habitat of complete indifference with everyone else will give way to complete order by itself as even the raging waters settle calmly like a clear mirror, the concept of not poking Your nose in other people's business will give complete liberty

As they are not responsible for You and You Yourself are not responsible for them just as there is no duty incumbent upon You there is no right incumbent upon them let them do as they please and they will let You do as You please, don't try to change their way by force and don't force them, they themselves can make a way out for themselves and look to improve Yourself and present Yourself as a such a model character that the vices which are present in them according to You will disappear as they find Your character marvelously alluring and You become the walking talking mirror image of an ideal being, which such views on changing others

and Yourself will eliminate causes of unrest which has risen due to the fo
rceful implementation of orders on those who do not submit to it,

## Act Yourself

 This ideal of being selfless and putting others before Your gain is the on
e of the most corrupting elements of society in reality everyone is compl
etely selfish except for someone exceptions and they all care more for t
heir own life than others but this false labeling which has deluded every
one into relying on others have caused great mischief

 and given rise to authoritarian systems acting on behalf of people and v
owing selfless devotion to them and instead of this they have made their
life even more miserable than it already was and discarding the nonexist
ent sacred trust which they have themselves swore to uphold only to giv
e them a solid reason to do as they wish for themselves,

This nearly nonexistent trait of selflessness should be named to the origi
nal trait of being selfish as no one absolutely no one aside from the very
few truly care for anyone else and this menacing idea of helping those u
nfortunate by making them follow a better way of life by changing degra
ding exploiting and forcing them from that which they used to follow so t
hat they might be happy and independent as the ones helping them has le
d to the worst crimes ever, You must realize that mist feel better by faili
ng at what they have chosen for themselves by themselves instead of su
cceeding at what other chosen on behalf of them as the illusion of free c
hoice is way better for them instead of a forced one as a farmer who had
 lived poor all his life working in the fields will detest being forced to be
rich and having to abandon that which he has done all his life,

Even forcing someone to go towards paradise when they have chosen he
ll for themselves will be more painful for them than burning there foreve
r, You must look only to Yourself and should not have any feeling of selfl
ess devotion to anyone else as they most certainly don't have any for Yo
u and Your sympathy would be more injurious to them than being comple
tely indifferent towards them as being ignorant and content is way more
better than knowing a lot and not being,

Let everyone choose their own path if they want themselves to be subse rvient to a group of people acting on their behalf let them if they want to be their own masters let them if they want equality and same for everyo ne as long as they do this with those that want them to do this to them,

And worrying about a complete split of communities because of such lib erty is self-destructive know that no two human beings can completely b e the same let everyone make their own world their own lifestyle own lik es and dislikes their own perception of good and evil their own ethical be liefs for every argument that exists there exists a completely opposite ar guments with the same level of logic and proofs but being completely ag ainst the first one, like the argument of being pro-life or pro-choice both of them have very strong basis and reasons but they stem from complet ely opposite ideals,

And the only solution to this or any other argument is that that anyone who supports it should follow it themselves and encourage other to follo w without forcing another's option being taken away, a utopian society is not that which lives according to one order but that all completely differ ent and opposing orders existing side by side without any of them affecti ng the others,

## Ethics

Ideals themselves are useless unless they are acted upon by someone an d some ideals are that which are barely impossible no matter how much work is done on them pursuing that which will most likely not be achieve d sets the standard for what is more likely to be achieved as he who kne w he can't say less to the sun and more to the rain lived happily and died not in vain,

Trying to go after that which is too good to be true causes much anguis h and sometimes a great reward is only a step away it's only Your thinki ng that determines the gain some win by losing others lose by winning al l that glitters is not gold or sometimes all the gold is not glitter,

There exist many views to a single sight as an unlimited number of lines can pass through a single point,

Think before You leap as what You see hear feel or think might not turn out to be the way You expected, The more You'll get to know the more Y ou'll understand that You know less and less,

Another misleading view that exists judge not and not be judged is a mai n cause of sadness instead of teaching everyone how to judge it is told t hat you must not judge at all, judging is a trait of the very basic human n ature and without judging one cannot even differentiate between black a nd white, and such absurd ideals are an integral part of the old orders,

whereas the more the person judges the more he knows about himself a s other people have same brain which is capable of nearly everything an d before judging another one must know that he himself is the way he is not because he individually thought of all that by himself without the ass ociation of another other but his entire personality is the result of all that he came in contact with and mainly the societal norms he adapted to by being exposed to that particular group for a long time,

Ideals don't but events do create the personality of a person and his acti ons are most certainly not always exactly as preached by the ideals that he follows, simply put ethics don't always co relate with belief the perso n has,

while keeping all this in mind it is evident that the personality of an indiv

idual is the collective result of all that he has come in contact with but m
ost especially the most influencing practices took a hold of him and made
up his personality as the child's behavior is the judge of the parents per
sonality, so are You that what You live through,

You should judge an individual based on what his personal ethics are not
based upon that which he claims to follow as stated in the 1st Syllable a
nd thinking that unrestraint in choosing a way of life will wreak havoc up
on the world is the thinking which is done by keeping the old orders in m
ind as the new world order or rightfully the Perfect World Order gives su
ch liberty that an individual will set their own ethics based on that which
they see as right not on the dictation of others

As the old orders propagates such absurdities that without dissociating Y
ourself from them and then looking at their corrupt inventions only then
You'll realize that You are being fooled on a grand scale along with every
one else into submitting into their so called order maintaining systems w
hich doesn't do that which they say but the complete opposite,

and they have established a monopoly over thought on the brain of nearl
y everyone and have prevented them from doing as they please for them
selves and caused great unhappiness, as happiness is not found by makin
g everyone live the same life but giving everyone the choice to make wh
at they want of their life by themselves as a fish in a small pond is more
free than a fish in a large aquarium,

Letting everyone feel that they themselves are doing all they want with t
heir life without external pressure gives them joy as the poor classes in
the old orders are unhappy with the rich as they are being forced into be
ing told what and what not to do while they perceive the rich to be compl
etely independent, and in between the rich exploit them in such a way th
at their right hand doesn't know what their left hand has lost,

and if they are left completely alone and dependent on themselves they
will make more out of their life than they'll ever make by being depende
nt on others,

When one realizes that no one really cares for him and he must take care of himself alone than he is of more potential and likely to accomplish mo re than those who are dependent even slightly on others as he'll have to carefully plan everything regarding his life by himself and not wait for th e help of others,

while those who rely on others giving them their own selves in bondage are more likely to be unhappy even if they accomplish something, for the ir success would not be completely theirs and if they do not succeed thei r all hopes and dreams become shattered and then they realizes if only t hey had not done so,

But all that which happened, happened the way it happened because it w ouldn't have happened any other way because it couldn't, and it is better to have suffered a big loss and forgotten about it than suffering a small l oss and thinking of it over and over again moving on and letting things g o is the way of life as in reality nothing is actually Yours,

You use it for some time and then You leave it forever and it comes in an other's possessions and being attached to things is not good at all liberty of thought being granted fully but utilized partially is an insult to liberty itself don't make Yourself the prisoner of Your own  thought learn to let go and do not pursue vain desires that will lead to Your own loss be selfl ess even though your basic nature is selfish and even though the entire c ommunity in itself be completely selfish do not be like them their desires dictate their ethics

Form Your own ideals and let them be Your guide above Your desires, an d think thoroughly about all that which happens around You or to You, as even Your one selfless act in the entire selfish community will have a pr ofound effect on all of them as none will be expecting anything at all and selfless acts in a society that realizes it's very nature as selfish and hav ing no notions of assistance without expectation of payment, will raise Y our rank way above all of them,

Even if You achieve all the wealth in the world use not all on Your own s elf but live for something greater than Yourself have a goal that which Y our being yearns to accomplish live for others even though they would n ot do the same for You remember just as You were born You will die but you can still leave a mark that will change the world for better,

Living a selfless life gives such happiness that even the strongest drugs cannot induce though while You might be taken for granted and will most certainly be exploited become not like them no matter what be prepared to be butchered rather than become the butcher Yourself and propose n ot such ideals which will make living harder for You and those who willfu lly submit to them but make life easier and jump not into doing something in rash decision but analyze, interpret and act accordingly taking not too long and not being rash and think in a long run instead of a short one as dime saved every day is worth ten times on the tenth day and sometimes that same dime well spent is better than the ten times the savings of ten th day, as there exists no absolute answer to anything and sometimes th e opposite of that which is generally taught and accepted is more fitting f or that particular event and sometimes the most simple answer does the trick simply put no ideal is specifically applicable in all situations and in all times

<u>Morality</u>

A trait that may be considered as a vice by many may be considered a virtue by others

There exists different perceptions of everything and these perceptions determine what is right and what is wrong and not all perceptions cover the entire view as they may be formed keeping a specific part of image in mind and ignoring the rest,

As these virtues may be considered as vices by others but in reality they may benefit an individual more than the harms others have purported to them to, following are the virtues which the others may see as vices an may see the antonyms of these traits as virtues instead of vices:

i) <u>Virtue of Lust</u>
It is a very powerful desire that curbing it causes agitation and decreases the efficiency of an individual instead this virtue must be utilized to its full extent and one must increase it in one's self and have great desire longing and yearning for it as only with its fulfillment will one gain satisfaction as opposed to its opposite Vice chastity and when it is pursued after causes great anxiety as it is the denial of something that is an essential requirement and is as basic as the need for food and water and going after the vice of chastity will give way to many more ills in society

ii) <u>Virtue of Gluttony</u>

It is an excellent trait as there are so many tasty foods to try and such a short life to try them in eating to an excess gives person the joy in satisfying their taste buds and in between this tasty process giving them a fuller figure which is viewed by some as an expression of wealth and good health whereas the vice of temperance which teaches restraint and not even trying to pursue all that one can in his life and causing a waste of a person's potential to try out new things making society come to a standstill by following it

iii) <u>Virtue of Greed</u>

One of the many driving forces for doing better than one is able to do onl y by the virtue of greed can someone attain such heights that he has wis hed to attain by asking and working for more and stopping at nothing les s than the very best, by striving for more and more and thus making the society better in itself and where as its opposite Vice of Charity which gi ves the false hope of benefit from a complete stranger and giving away t he hard earned wealth that one has acquired by the labor of his being to those who hide behind the mask of desperation and misery like a parasit e sucking the blood and still being thin as a hair such vice has altered th e mentality of many instead for striving for themselves but relying on oth ers

iv) <u>Virtue of Sloth</u>

Should be set as a goal which one should try to achieve by the Virtue of Greed when one has made himself excel way above others then in this vi rtue is one of his best friends having all and everything being taken care for him by only by the expenditure of his wealth and giving him contentm ent later in life where as the Vice of Diligence is like a rust on an iron no matter how expensive it is slowly it is eaten away by over exerting one' s self and this pitiful vice has caused many to not enjoy life and waste th eir life worrying about that which should not even matter

v) <u>Virtue of Wrath</u>

Is a natural trait which should be harnessed and used appropriately as it not only makes another see the wrong that he has done but also gives th e one who has been wronged a sense of relief and giving him a lower mu ch calmer state after a higher frustrated one, virtue of wrath should open ly be expressed as it not only does justice for the one who has been wro nged but also provides an example to others hindering them from doing b ad and to consider wrath an evil and give priority to the vice of kindness more creates more evil than good in the society as it stops the anger fro m letting out when it was mild and thus it accumulates over time and eat s the person from within

vi) Virtue of Envy

Is one of the  qualities in the basic nature and it is best fueled by virtue of greed desiring something that someone else has and with greed desiring something that all others have should be used as a driving force in the betterment of a person's personal character as one sees another with great accomplishment and wish the same for himself so he might become as better as the others and make society even better and reducing the ills that already plague it and urging all others to do the same whereas the vice of kindness giving others something for no return diminishes the very hope of progress and advancement in society as one seeks that by only the vice of kindness he might exploit others in to giving him something just because he appears as less rich than others is a vice which is against the harmony of a progressive society

vii) Virtue of Pride

The last virtue in which a person can boast and display all that he has achieved and earned to others and having faith in his own abilities which encourages all others following the virtues of greed and envy they see the prideful as a goal that they must accomplish and showing to the society that if the prideful have achieved so much so can the others do the same by following all that they show off whereas the vice of humility not only eradicates the force behind work and progress but also encourages the one who has done less for himself and even less for society to be content with his lowly state and pursue not that which should be pursued and ending the very basic quality of human beings to strive and struggle be better and show it to others causing one of the worst corruptions in society

## Critique

The traits which have been mentioned were explained the one sided men tality of the old orders,

Which look at only some part of the details and ignore the rest even the worst vices if implemented carefully are better than the beat virtues impl emented carelessly,

 it is all an instance of mind over matter everything is as good and as ba d as one wants to be,

And giving complete moral authority to do as they wish to any order can hinder an entire civilization's progress,

And making everyone give allegiance to the same ideal causes the ideal i tself to. Implode from within because of its refusal to see consider anoth er part of the argument as an ideal refuses to consider any other opposin g doctrine even into consideration so should You refuse to consider their self-claimed supremacy as absolute, but as worthless as popped up timb er,

Don't confine Your mind from exploring other possibilities to a given situ ation as sometimes that which seems to be damaging may heal and that which seems to heal may damage,

Nothing is as it seems and sometimes there is nothing to it except the w ay it seems,

Explore new horizons and You'll find something way better than Your cur rent life style

And as You'll know more and more the less and less You'll understand an d the more You'll understand the more You'll know, but You are prevente d from knowing another's perspective as they have been dubbed lower t han the lowest low in the lowest part of the Your artificially divided com munity,

The followers of the old orders have made sure to prevent any means by which their chains of oppression may become loose and have underlined and organized in such an excellent way that any disunited ideals of liberty that try to break independent from it their chains are eradicated even before they are even born,

And short periods of aimless independence that have emerged in various place have been brought down as they were not thought of thoroughly they had no firm starting pointing and no firm plan in case their supports are broken

## The Scheme

The process of Liberty must be clearly defined and liberty is nothing les
s than liberty any conditions to curb it to allow its continuity is an artifici
al contract and not liberty itself,

Knowing what liberty is, is not enough, but also how to pursue it, get it a
nd the hardest part maintain it and be prepared to make sure that it is no
t compromised in any way by knowing the entire scheme thoroughly and
implementing it step by step with a backup plan in every case and keepin
g in mind the every possible outcome

## A) Begin Your struggle

The most important stage in the entire scheme is that first the mind must
be liberated in the very beginning by firmly holding on to The Syllables,
and realizing all forms of subjugations and unconscious manipulations, kn
owing that Your mind itself is the foundation of liberty,

and You must not accept any artificial form of segregation in whatever f
orm that may be, in which You Yourself are presented to Yourself as bel
onging to a superior community way above all others and You must not r
ecognize any boundaries between the human such based on caste, color,
creed, tongue, culture, ideals or nationality as these are nothing but label
s which have been given to individuals to give them a sense of belonging
to a community and none of these labels can alter the fact that everyone
has the same potential of molding himself into a particular character me
aning the entire human community is one and the differences that exists
are one of the main cause in making a utopian society and must be embr
aced instead of being shunned neglected or frowned upon as everyone is
equal but unique and this uniqueness is his own identity

## B) Propagate liberty

After the great realization in Yourself You must tell it to others that they
might not be a slave anyone of an elaborate web of deceit in their own m

ind and explain to them in such a kind manner that they themselves wish to know more of it and to be a part of the struggle liberating themselves and liberating others You must not spare any effort in letting others know about as their liberty depends upon You

## C) Unite the liberators

As more and more people become aware of their slavery without consent they will have developed a completely new perspective of their surrounding You must unite with them in Your struggle against oppressions and clearly know that You have one main goal of liberty after that everyone goes their own way owing to their uniqueness but during the initial stage or the last stage You must not resort to force in any circumstance and work together in a completely peaceful manner

## D) Demand Your right

As the suppressing orders demand that You all be divided and not live in harmony employing the use of force,

You must do the same except for the force part and struggle for Your right of independence to do as You please not be puppets whose string and pulled twisted cut and then it is thrown out You have one right by Your birth of personal choice and that exists not until bit exists You are merely told that You are independent but that independence comes with a leash that is shortened and shortened You should not back down no matter what happens

## E) Reject Any compromise

As they are not willing to even just a basic right of choice and curbing it is the violation of liberty itself as any compromise will only mean the continuation of old orders, It must be rejected without hesitation and not to be considered,

Only applicable scenario for an independent mind is Liberty or Death, as liberty is life and there is nothing else to life other than death,

And have no fear in standing up for what You believe in as one who stan ds up for anything doesn't fall down for everything and death should not be frowned upon as it is the ultimate pleasure the most relaxed time of li fe is sleep and what's more relaxing than its permanent continuity,

Your liberated mind must not fear anything but embrace all that which is to come

F) <u>Repel the attacks</u>

When the enforcers of the old orders fail to make You submit into recogn izing their self-made supreme authority they will try to kill You or as the y'll dub it, restoring the calm, getting rid of the rebels, ensuring peace an d such blatant lies only to support their finite order that will eventually b e crushed with time,

Use of force is only permitted when it is used by the others first but it s hould be noted that in this scenario it should only be used to repel the sa vagery if there is a fair chance of triumph otherwise it will be the death of You and complete massacre of liberators

G) <u>Stalemate of power</u>

This situation will arise when their attacks have been repelled one by on e and many are united for their right to pursue their own ideals,

You must not engage in merry making just yet as this is one of the most crucial steps in the cycle, You must ensure by means of peace that all th ose who are still unwillingly subjugated may demand their rights as well and then the oppressor's pyramid of power will start to collapse from wit hin,

And with Your continued effort towards their liberation they will eventua lly become as independent as is guaranteed by the Syllables

H) <u>Abolishment of all forms of restrictions</u>

After they have been thoroughly defeated it must be ensured that no ord er be allowed to do anything with others without their will and as for thei r continuation all those that willfully want to follow it are allowed as long as their ideals so not physically interfere with the syllables

And the most important part in this step to ensure that all property claim ed in the name of people dubbed as public property which is only a cover ing to ensure orders supremacy must be abolished without any exception

And unoccupied land is his who builds their first, no one is allowed to cla im unoccupied land without having the immediate resources of building s omething there and unoccupied land is without any cost anyone who buil ds something somewhere that place belongs to him

And as for the question of roads they too shall be privatized and recogni zed as the property of he who builds it and he is allowed to do as he wis h with that road

And the intellectual property is the sole responsibility of the creator it's his duty to do as he wish with it and his inability to do so must not be bla med on anyone else and no one is allowed to prosecute others for the inf ringing the rights of intellectual property thereof because there exists no rights for such property and the safest way for it to be preserved is to b e not created in the first place it's the very own creation makes the crea tor liable for its safeguarding, implementation and regulation and no else as stated in the 1st Syllable,

As for the inventions that will be left behind by the old orders such as bu ildings, money and equipment's will be destroyed unless the liberators ta ke a hold of such things by themselves and do as they please with it

And the armies that will be left behind will have their shackles removed and entire armies will be disbanded and no public army will exist if some one wishes to make his personal army than he is allowed to do so

The weapons that will be left behind should be destroyed by the liberato

rs and any new weapons that will be made will be the sole property of th
e owner and no one has the authority to take them away no matter what
they support their claim with as stated in the 3rd Syllable

I) Laws and their regulations

Aside from the three syllables no one has the authority to see to the impl
ementation of anything on anyone else without their will and there will n
ot be any limits imposed on anyone without them imposing it on their sel
ves by their selves and for their selves

And no matter if even 99 people want a limit imposed on the 100th they
are not allowed to do with him as they please as they would not like him
to do with them as he pleases,

And all forms of limits stylishly fashioned as laws in the hope of curbing
individual liberty and identity unto that of cattle and herding them where
ver they want if anyone wants to pursue such a system he is allowed to
do as he please and submit himself to any ideals he wishes to and if any
exceeds the bound then all and everyone beside him have the duty to im
plement use of the 3rd Syllable for the one affected in the manner he so
shall desire

J) Discontent and disorders

With the implementation of Liberty some ideals will grow very stronger t
hat all others are dwarfed by them

And they'll might will grow so big that they'll have the power to do as th
ey please without the consideration of The Three Syllables and the migh
t of all those who will try to stop them will be of no match and the power
ful order will be victorious and after the victory it will be ensured that no
other ideal be allowed to exist and systematic eradication of Liberty will
begin by cunning persuasion and use of force where ever applicable and
thus rendering the liberators to a mere fraction of what they'll used to b
e

## K) Ending and the beginning

Nothing is forever, the liberators once having ultimate independence will slowly be imprisoned again and will disappear and so will the order that caused all of this as it was once weak and so will it become again weak

And start to crumble as variants of it will arise as an ideal is only the same ideal if changed by the creator or by whom the creator has given the authority to do so otherwise anyone else changing it creates a split from the original ideal and forms a new one having no relation to the former even if the editor claims it to be,

After their crumble chaos will rain again and again will the liberators get the power to put things aright this cycle will repeat again and again sometimes terminating in the beginning sometimes the middle and sometimes the end its only Your belief in it that will keep it existing,

As Your breathing continues Your existence so does belief continue an ideal's existence and as soon as the last person stops believing in that ideal the ideal seizes to exist but no matter what ever happens a cycle once started continues forever

## Foundation

This entire Cycle should be thoroughly understood and firmly grasped

And hope must not be abandoned even if the situations look grim as even the arrow need to be pulled back before it is launched

Your determination and steadfastness is the key in achieving Your very own liberty in all its forms because without it Your thought expressions and actions all are limited and You are a prisoner who has been given a li fe sentence of slavery just because of the event of Your birth,

And their only argument is that their system has been set in place becau se their way of order is the only answer to life

Whereas the answer of life is there is no answer,

And any else answer You think up of is Yours to follow and of those who would willfully follow You, all that one would ever need to know about li berty has been explained and in the briefest way possible so that its me morization will be easy for all

And only with liberty will everyone have an opportunity to think as they would like to think to express as they would like to express and to act as they would like to express without worrying about any restrictions bein g imposed on them and giving each and every one such great power that was not even dreamt of before, reshaping the fate of every single organi sm there is and will be and giving such contentment to every single one t hat one might wonder if the world itself is the promised paradise, and ma king the possibility of every opportunity to turn into success because of this Perfect World Order, As of now Your mind has been liberated and it' s a matter of time before everyone is liberated as well

*Long Live Liberty*

www.ingramcontent.com/pod-product-compliance
Lightning Source LLC
Chambersburg PA
CBHW060020300526
45794CB00003B/1235